Tom Gidwitz

Story in the Stone

The Formation of a Tropical Land Bridge

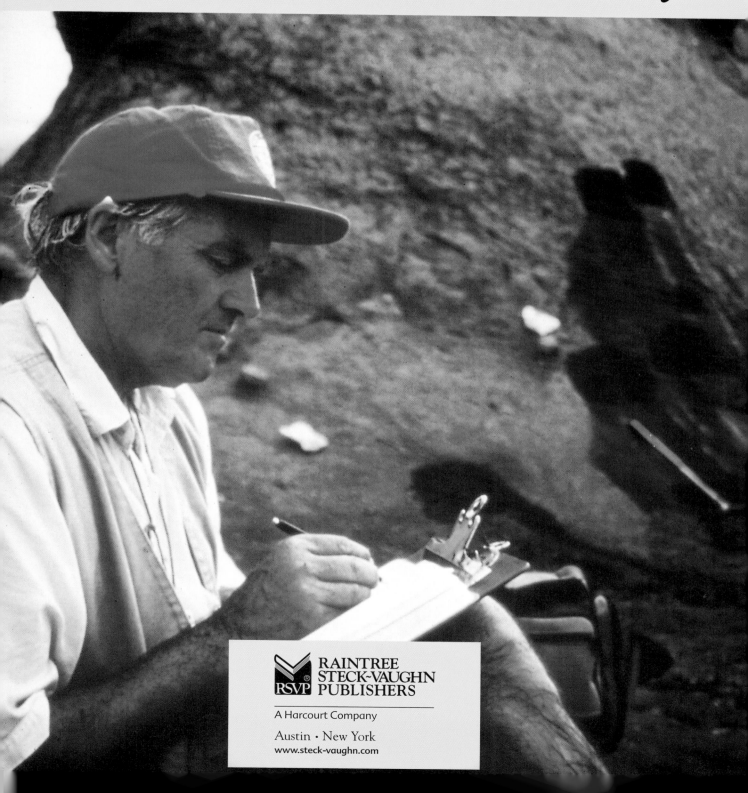

RSVP®
RAINTREE
STECK-VAUGHN
PUBLISHERS

A Harcourt Company

Austin · New York
www.steck-vaughn.com

For my parents

Steck-Vaughn Company

First published 2001 by Raintree Steck-Vaughn Publishers,
an imprint of Steck-Vaughn Company.

Copyright © 2001 Turnstone Publishing Group, Inc.
Copyright © 2001, text, by Tom Gidwitz.

Library of Congress Cataloging-in-Publication Data

Gidwitz, Tom.
  Story in the stone: the formation of a tropical land bridge / Tom Gidwitz.
    p. cm. — (Rain forest pilot)
  Includes bibliographical references and index.
  ISBN 0-7398-2217-9 (hardcover)   ISBN 0-7398-2226-8 (softcover)
  1. Geology — Panama — Panama, Isthmus of — Juvenile literature.
[1. Panama, Isthmus of (Panama) 2. Geology. 3. Geologists. 4. Paleontology.]
I. Title. II. Series.
QE216.G53 2000
557.287—dc21   00-029123

For information about this and other Turnstone reference books and
educational materials, visit Turnstone Publishing Group on the World Wide
Web at http://www.turnstonepub.com.

  Photo and illustration credits listed on page 48 constitute part of this
copyright page.

Printed and bound in the United States of America.

1 2 3 4 5 6 7 8 9 0 LB 05 04 03 02 01 00

Contents

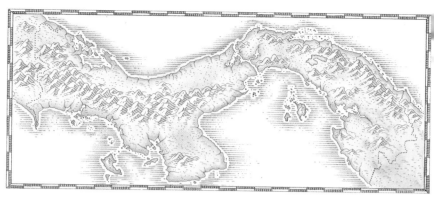

1 Tony's Team

When volcanoes erupt, they shoot out lava and ash. Eruptions can cause damage and injury. But volcanoes do other things, too. They played a part in forming the Isthmus of Panama.

Ash rises from the Cerro Negro volcano, blocking the sun. The earth shakes. The mountain thunders. In villages below the volcano, families pack their belongings and flee. Hot orange lava spills down the volcano's sides. Within moments, the lava turns black as it begins to cool into solid rock.

Cerro Negro is in Nicaragua, a country on the Isthmus (pronounced "ISS-muhs") of Panama. The isthmus is a thin piece of land that joins North America and South America. It is geologically active. That means it is a place where volcanoes erupt and earthquakes shake the ground. More than 30 of the 350 volcanoes there have erupted in the past 500 years. But 300 miles southeast of Cerro Negro, all is quiet in Panama. The wind is warm. The sea is calm. Pelicans glide from the tops of palm trees. They land lightly on the water.

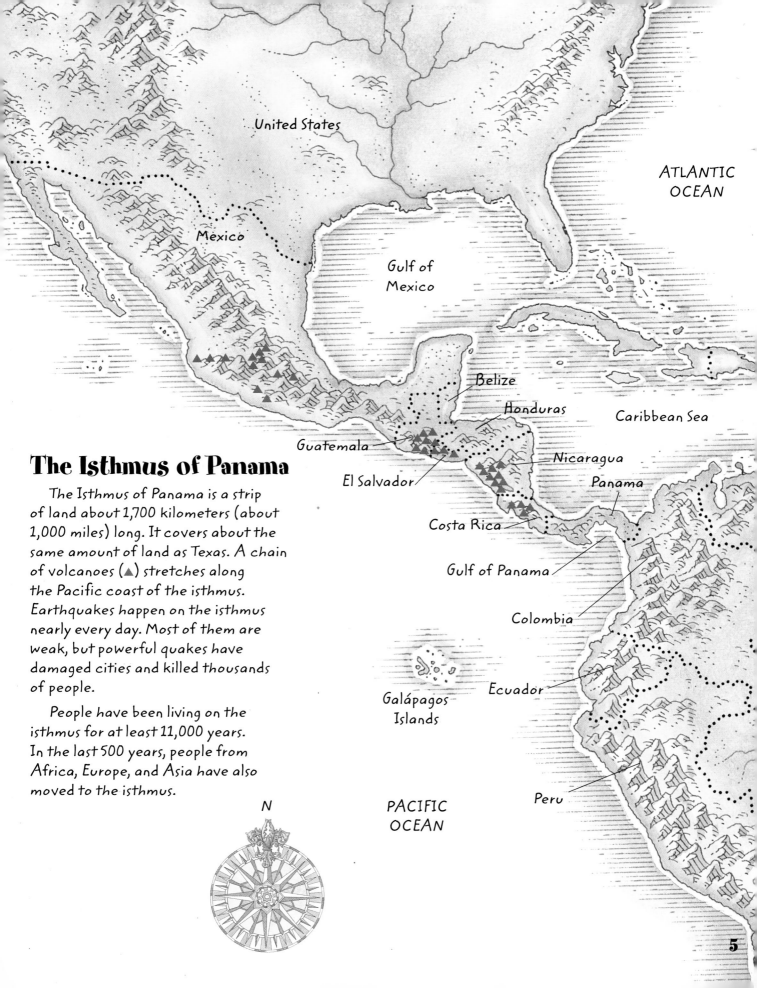

United States

ATLANTIC OCEAN

Mexico

Gulf of Mexico

Belize

Honduras

Caribbean Sea

Guatemala

Nicaragua

El Salvador

Panama

Costa Rica

Gulf of Panama

Colombia

Ecuador

Galápagos Islands

Peru

PACIFIC OCEAN

N

The Isthmus of Panama

The Isthmus of Panama is a strip of land about 1,700 kilometers (about 1,000 miles) long. It covers about the same amount of land as Texas. A chain of volcanoes (▲) stretches along the Pacific coast of the isthmus. Earthquakes happen on the isthmus nearly every day. Most of them are weak, but powerful quakes have damaged cities and killed thousands of people.

People have been living on the isthmus for at least 11,000 years. In the last 500 years, people from Africa, Europe, and Asia have also moved to the isthmus.

Here Tony Coates and two other scientists are hard at work. They stand in shallow water at the edge of a small island. In front of them is a low, striped cliff. The scientists use hammers and other tools to chip at a gray stripe, or layer, in the cliff. Inside the layer are the remains of small animals called corals that lived two million years ago. These remains, like the buried remains of plants and other animals, are called fossils.

Looking at Layers

The island where Tony and his team of scientists are working is called Swan Cay (pronounced KEY). Swan Cay is only 16 kilometers (10 miles) from the isthmus. It is one of many islands that are part of the area called Bocas del Toro, or "Mouths of the Bull." Tony and his team of scientists often work on Swan Cay and the other islands of Bocas.

Tony and his team often work along the shore. At the ocean's edge, waves wear away the land. This can expose rock layers and fossils that are millions of years old.

CARIBBEAN SEA

Bocas del Toro

Panama City

GULF OF PANAMA

Panama

Swan Cay is covered with green plants. So are the other islands and the mainland. But beneath the palm trees and tropical plants, there are layers of rock. Rock layers can be seen on mountainsides and in riverbeds. They are also found along cliffs and places where rock is cut to make roads.

Some of these layers of rock were formed by lava, like the lava that erupted from Cerro Negro. Other layers were once mud or sand. The layers hold fossils of fish, clams, snails, and animals and plants too tiny to see.

Tony wants to know what materials are in each layer and how they combined to make the layer. Each layer holds clues that can tell Tony about the formation of the isthmus and everything on it. What Tony finds out about the past can help him understand more about the isthmus today.

(above)
Bocas del Toro includes dozens of islands. Together they have hundreds of kilometers of shoreline. There, Tony and his team can see more layers of fossils and rocks than almost anywhere else on the isthmus.

(below)
This is part of Swan Cay. Swan Cay is one of the smaller islands in Bocas.

The Panama Paleontology Project

Tony is a geologist. A geologist is a scientist who studies the history of Earth, what it's made of, and how it formed. Tony is a kind of geologist called a paleontologist. A paleontologist learns about Earth by studying fossils.

Tony and his fellow scientist Jeremy Jackson work as paleontologists with the Smithsonian Tropical Research Institute (STRI) in Panama. They have put together a team of scientists to help understand the history of the isthmus. This team is part of the Panama Paleontology Project, or PPP, which includes more than 30 scientists from all around the world.

They come to Panama because the Bocas islands and the isthmus itself hold more fossils than anyone can count. And the fossils have been there for tens of millions of years.

Collecting Samples

To find out about the isthmus, Tony needs to collect many samples, or small amounts of material. For this, he often travels to Bocas. On this trip, he is joined by Nancy Budd and Steve Cairns, who are experts on fossilized corals. Nancy is a professor at the University of Iowa. Over the past six years, she has collected more than 5,000 coral fossils in Jamaica, Costa Rica, and Panama. "Bocas is one of the best-known places in the world for finding fossils of corals that lived two million years ago," she says.

Steve began collecting fossils when he was ten years old. Now he studies corals at the Smithsonian Institution in Washington, D.C.

On this trip, Tony, Nancy, and Steve spend more than one week collecting samples at Bocas. At night they work, eat, and sleep at a field station in Bahia Azul, a village in Bocas. The field station is built on stilts over the water. The village has no roads or cars, so each morning the scientists travel to work in a speedboat.

Tony, Nancy, and Steve chip samples from layers of rock using hammers and other tools. They put each sample into a different bag. On each bag they write a number. In a notebook they write the place, the date, and a description of the rocks in which the sample was found.

(above)
Tony and his team head out for a day of sample collecting. The building behind them is the Bahia Azul field station.

(below)
Nancy chips off a sample from a rock layer. She'll place the sample in the bag she's holding and then label the bag.

(inset)
The scientists put each sample they collect into a bag like this one.

(above)
Sometimes getting the bagged samples back to the boat can be tricky.

What the scientists find on trips like this one can be very important. They are interested in the fossils of plants and animals that once lived in the oceans, on the seafloor, or along the shore. Some of the samples they collect offer clues to the history of the isthmus. Others help scientists decide how old different parts of the isthmus are.

Scientists also examine minerals, or nonliving material, in the layers where the fossils are found. Each fossil and bit of material could be an important clue. Someday these clues will help Tony and his team explain how the isthmus formed.

Bringing Home the Evidence

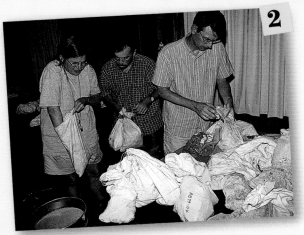

At the end of the collecting trip, Nancy, John Dawson, and Steve unpack all the bags of samples.

At the end of each day in Bahía Azul, Tony checks the samples to make certain they are labeled correctly. He also makes notes in his field notebook about the day's work.

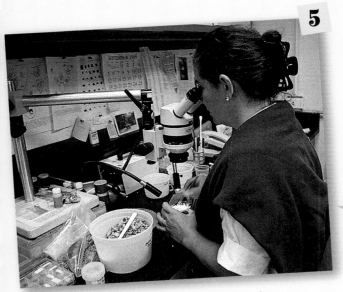

Here, John and Tony sort through the samples they have collected.

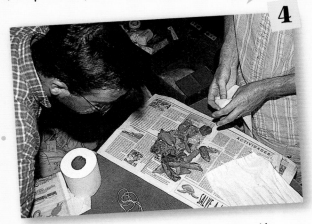

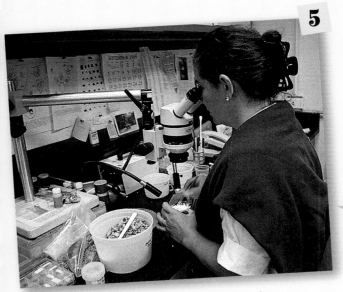

At the STRI laboratory, technicians like Yira Ventocilla, above, clean, identify, sort, and measure the samples. They also compare the samples to those collected on other trips.

Finally, the scientists carefully wrap the samples in tissue paper. Then, they put each wrapped sample in a small can. Some samples are sent to the scientists' laboratories, and some are sent to STRI's laboratory for study.

2 The Isthmus Is Rising

Fossil samples like these can help scientists understand how Earth formed.

Tony and his team can't examine the whole isthmus to find out what they want to know. It's too big, and they can't reach all the layers. So they take samples at certain places. That's what Tony, Nancy, and Steve did at Bocas. Tony uses the information that he and other scientists collect to make a picture of the rock layers. The picture is called a section. The scientists label each layer in the section based on the type of rock it contains. Looking at sections from different places helps Tony see how the layers fit together.

Some sections show layers with fossils. The fossils include shark teeth, fish bones, shells, corals, and tiny plants and animals.

The kinds of fossils Tony finds are like the materials that settle to the ocean floor today. That makes Tony think that the layers with fossils were once at the bottom of the ocean, too. But today, some of the layers he studies are high overhead. How did they get there? The layers can only be above sea level now if something from below lifted them. If the layers rose, the whole isthmus must have risen. In fact, the isthmus is still rising. What is causing it to rise?

Looking at Layers

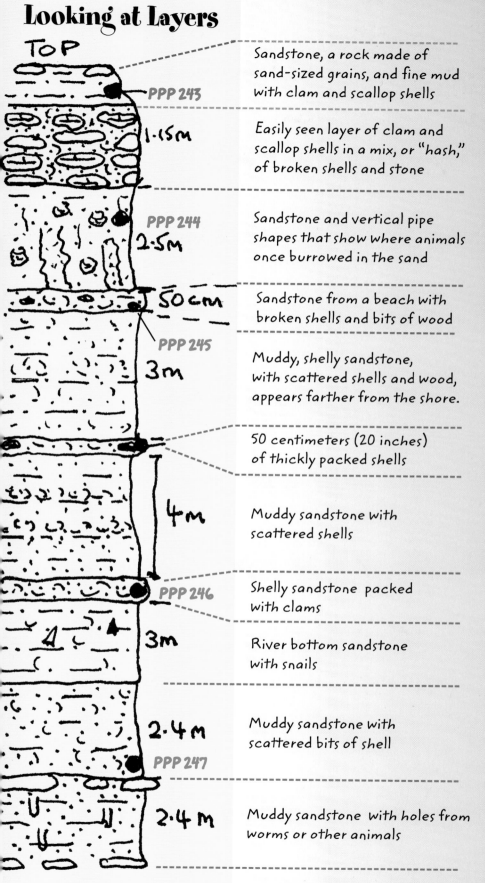

TOP

PPP 243 — Sandstone, a rock made of sand-sized grains, and fine mud with clam and scallop shells

1·15m — Easily seen layer of clam and scallop shells in a mix, or "hash," of broken shells and stone

PPP 244 — Sandstone and vertical pipe
2·5m — shapes that show where animals once burrowed in the sand

50cm — Sandstone from a beach with broken shells and bits of wood

PPP 245 — Muddy, shelly sandstone,
3m — with scattered shells and wood, appears farther from the shore.

50 centimeters (20 inches) of thickly packed shells

4m — Muddy sandstone with scattered shells

PPP 246 — Shelly sandstone packed with clams

3m — River bottom sandstone with snails

2·4m — Muddy sandstone with scattered bits of shell

PPP 247

2·4m — Muddy sandstone with holes from worms or other animals

Shell "hash"

Fossil layers

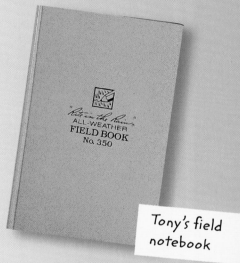

Tony's field notebook

Tony numbers each place he visits and each sample he collects. He also draws a map of each place in his field notebook. He makes a picture, called a section, of the layers that he can see. Then, he adds the sample numbers, such as PPP 243, to the section. The layers in this section from El Macho Creek in Golfo Dulce, Costa Rica, are 20 meters tall (about 65 feet). They are from about one million years old at the top to about one and one-half million years old at the bottom.

13

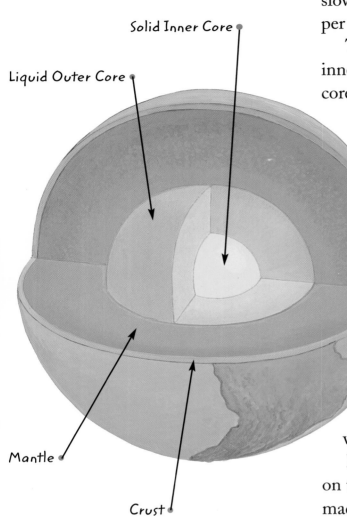

Solid Inner Core

Liquid Outer Core

Mantle

Crust

Earth is layered like a giant jawbreaker. It has a core, a mantle, and a surface crust.

Beneath Your Feet

It may be hard to believe, but the ground we walk on moves. The movement is usually very, very slow, sometimes only 2.5 centimeters (about 1 inch) per year. Why does it move?

The main answer is heat that comes from the inner parts of Earth. Scientists think that Earth's core is about 4,700°C (about 8,500°F). This heat moves out from Earth's core into the mantle.

The mantle is a hot layer. It surrounds the outer part of the core. The top of the mantle is partly melted. Heat from the core makes this melted part of the mantle move.

Think of the mantle as a pot of boiling water. As water in the bottom of the pot warms, it moves to the top. At the top, it cools and sinks back down. At the bottom, the water warms and rises again. Heat from the core makes the melted part of the mantle move up and down in the same way. But it happens very slowly.

Earth's outer layer is called the crust. We walk on the crust. It also forms the seafloor. The crust is made of huge slabs of rock called plates. The plates ride on the melted mantle. As the melted mantle moves, the plates move. And it's all because of the heat at the center of Earth.

Moving Plates

Plates move on the mantle like giant bumper cars in super slow motion. They move apart. They crash together. Or they slide past each other. This movement is called plate tectonics, and it's what causes land like the isthmus to rise from the oceans.

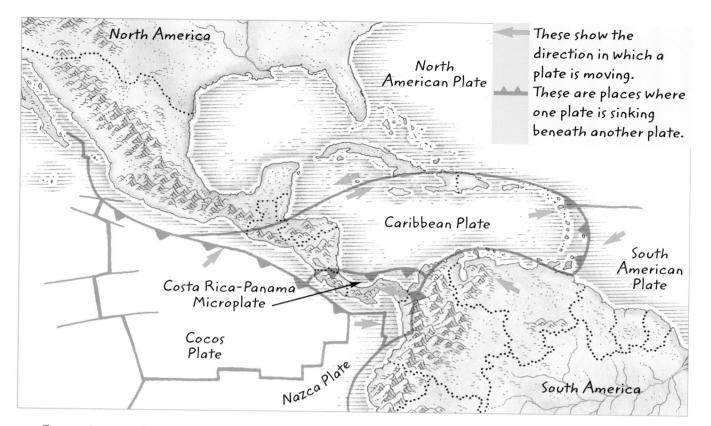

North America

North American Plate

These show the direction in which a plate is moving.
These are places where one plate is sinking beneath another plate.

Caribbean Plate

South American Plate

Costa Rica-Panama Microplate

Cocos Plate

Nazca Plate

South America

Sometimes when two plates move toward each other, they bump together. What happens next can depend on the density of each plate. Density is a measurement of the amount of matter in a particular amount of space. For example, steel is denser than plastic. A baseball made from steel would be denser and heavier than a baseball made from plastic.

When two plates bump together, sometimes the denser plate sinks beneath the less dense plate. Some of the rock in the sinking plate melts. If this melted rock moves up, it can erupt to form volcanoes. This is how the Isthmus of Panama formed. An ocean plate sank under the Caribbean Plate. Then, melted rock erupted and made the islands that would become the isthmus.

Plates can also move in other ways. They can slide past or pull away from each other. Each kind of plate movement has a different result.

Earth's crust is made of large and small plates that fit together like pieces in a puzzle. Near the Isthmus of Panama, five plates and one microplate, or small plate, are moving in different directions at different speeds. The movements of some of these plates caused the isthmus to form.

Plate Tectonics

Plate movements happen all over the world as plates bump, slide, sink, and pull apart. The word "tectonics" comes from an ancient Greek word that means carpenter or builder. Plate tectonics shape Earth's continents and oceans. It built the world we know today.

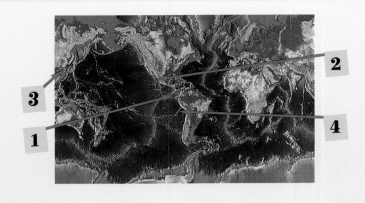

3

2

1

4

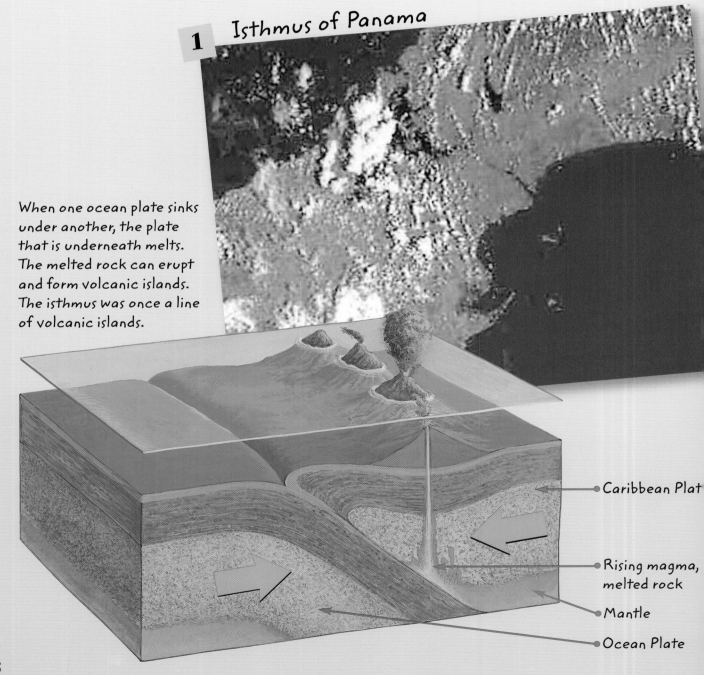

1 Isthmus of Panama

When one ocean plate sinks under another, the plate that is underneath melts. The melted rock can erupt and form volcanic islands. The isthmus was once a line of volcanic islands.

Caribbean Plat

Rising magma, melted rock

Mantle

Ocean Plate

2

When two plates slide past each other, earthquakes can happen. Earthquakes often shake Southern California as the North American and Pacific plates slide past each other. Here you can see the edges of the two moving plates.

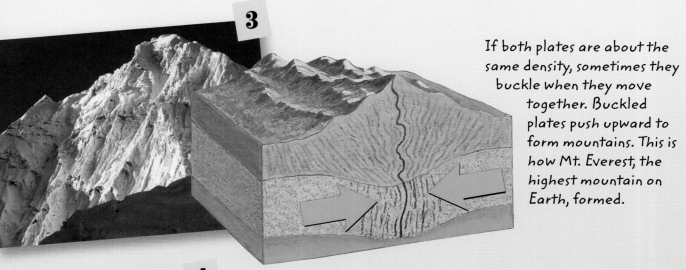

3

If both plates are about the same density, sometimes they buckle when they move together. Buckled plates push upward to form mountains. This is how Mt. Everest, the highest mountain on Earth, formed.

4

As plates pull apart, melted rock in the mantle oozes up, making new seafloor. At the edges of these plates are places where warm water rises out of cracks in the seafloor. The picture at left shows a cloud of heated water rising from one of these cracks.

Supercontinent

Today there are seven continents on Earth. But there haven't always been seven. Because of plate tectonics, Earth's continents have moved for billions of years. Geologists believe that about 260 million years ago, Earth's continents were joined. They formed one continent some scientists call Pangaea. Then, about 180 million years ago, Pangaea began to break apart.

Earth's continents were joined 260 million years ago in a "supercontinent" called Pangaea.

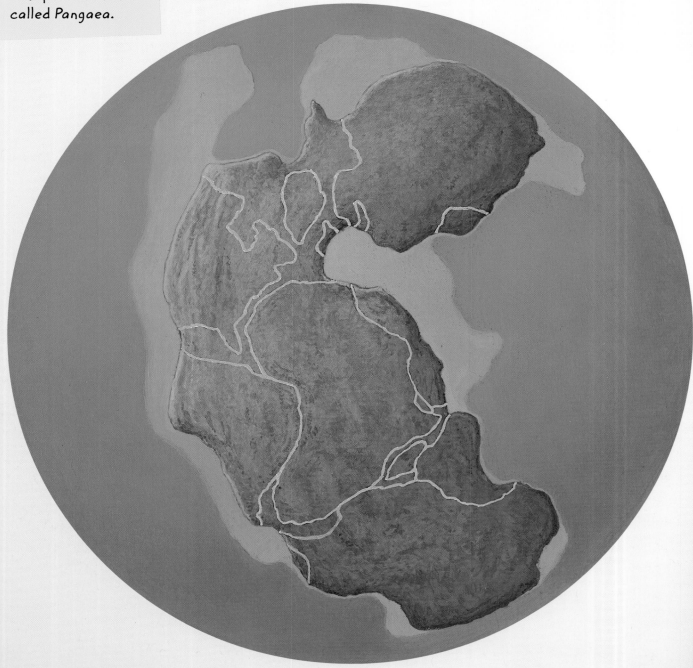

Slowly Pangaea began to split apart into separate continents.

This is the way Earth's continents look now.

First, North America separated from Europe, North Africa, and South America. As the plates pulled apart, the Atlantic Ocean formed. At that time, there was a wide opening between North and South America. The Atlantic and Pacific Oceans met in this opening. Then, about 80 million years ago, North and South America began to move together.

Over the next 60 million years, the Pacific and Caribbean plates bumped together. Where the plates met, volcanoes erupted. These volcanoes grew and formed islands. As the plates moved, so did the islands. These islands filled the space between North and South America. The story of the isthmus had begun.

3 Telltale Fossils

Tony wants to know how much older the cliff in the box on the left is than the cliff in the box on the right. The cliffs are part of the coastline at Wild Cane Cay. The cay is in Bocas del Toro.

Over the past 15 years, Tony has walked hundreds of kilometers, mapping and sampling rock layers. He has drawn many sections of rock, but he has not yet learned what he wants to know.

Tony wants to understand the history of the isthmus. Where did it start to form, and when? How fast did it rise? Where did the space between the Atlantic and Pacific Oceans begin to close? And how long ago did this happen? The answers to these questions can be found in the thousands of layers of rock and fossils on the isthmus.

If Tony identifies and compares different layers, he may be able to understand how quickly different parts of the isthmus rose out of the ocean. The different layers might also give clues about where and when the opening between the Atlantic and Pacific Oceans closed.

Tony needs to know two things about the different layers. First, when did each layer form? Second, where, or how deep in the ocean, did each layer form? To answer these questions, Tony turns to the members of his team for help.

Fossil Teamwork

Laurie Collins is a member of Tony's team. She studies the fossils of animals called benthic foraminifera. Foraminifera, or forams for short, are very tiny animals that live in the water. The word "benthic" means bottom living. So benthic forams are very tiny animals that live at the bottom of bodies of water.

Laurie studies benthic forams that have lived during the past 25 million years. She brings their shells home from the isthmus in small bags of sediment. Sediment is material that's found at the bottom of rivers and ponds and on the seafloor. It's made of mud, broken shells, and material that has dropped down through the layers of water. "It's not unusual to find 100 different kinds of benthic forams in a handful of ocean sediment," Laurie says.

The forams Laurie studies are the size of sand grains. But the most amazing thing about them is their shells. "They look like ornaments," she says. "They're so pretty. Some have long spines; others almost sparkle."

Laurie has collected more than 1,000 different kinds of benthic forams from different places on the isthmus. She has collected some forams that have never been seen before. Laurie's forams are a big help to Tony. They help him figure out where in the ocean the different isthmus layers formed.

When she was a child, Laurie Collins collected pretty rocks. She would wonder, "Where do these rocks come from? Why are these rocks different?" Laurie still asks those questions. But now she finds the answers in a lab at Florida International University, where she studies fossils.

They can help because benthic forams are fussy about where they live. Some kinds of benthic forams live on the seafloor, where the water is cold. Other kinds live in sand near the beach. The water there is warm and salty.

Benthic forams' fussiness is useful. Laurie can look at a benthic foram and tell Tony where it used to live. She can tell him if it lived in warm, shallow water or deep, cold water. With this information, Tony can determine how deep the layer that held the foram was when it formed.

Frozen Clocks

Laurie's studies help Tony know *where* a layer formed. To learn *when* a layer formed, Tony gets help from other researchers. Marie-Pierre Aubry is a scientist at Rutgers University, and her husband, Bill Berggren, is a scientist at the Woods Hole Oceanographic Institution in Woods Hole, Massachusetts. They have worked together for 20 years. They study the fossilized shells of plankton. Plankton are tiny plants and animals that float in the ocean.

"Plankton that drift in the ocean spread everywhere," Tony explains. "When the plankton die, they slowly sink. They then become part of the sediment."

The kind of plankton found in sediment from one layer can be different from the kind of plankton in a layer that is just a few hundred thousand years older. One hundred thousand years may sound like a long time, but to geologists, it's a short time.

When Marie-Pierre and Bill look at the fossil shells of plankton in a layer, they can tell how long ago the plankton lived. It is as if they are looking at a clock. But the clock has stopped ticking.

Fussy Forams

Benthic forams may be tiny, but their amazing shapes and patterns can be seen under a microscope.

From benthic foram shells in a rock layer, Laurie can determine at what depth the layer formed. Tony can use this information to compare different rock layers.

This shell is from a kind of benthic foram that usually lives at depths greater than 200 meters (about 650 feet).

This shell is from a kind of benthic foram that lives at depths of about 150 to 2,000 meters (about 500 to 6,500 feet).

From left to right, Marie-Pierre Aubry, Bill Berggren, paleontologist Jeremy Jackson, and Tony are studying a 12-million-year-old layer of volcanic lava at Bocas.

Small and Smaller

Bill and Marie-Pierre study different kinds of fossils. Bill studies forams called planktonic forams. They are forams that float. Like the forams Laurie studies, planktonic forams are tiny animals with beautiful shells.

Bill and other scientists have written a guide to identify and date many forams that lived between 65 and 55 million years ago. There are other guides to other time periods, too. Researchers keep these guides near their microscopes. When they find forams, they use the guides to tell them when the forams lived.

The forams Bill studies are small, but they are 100 times larger than the plankton Marie-Pierre studies. She studies nannoplankton. Each nannoplankton is so tiny that it is less than half the thickness of a human hair.

"The amazing thing is how small they are," Marie-Pierre says. To look at a fossil of a nannoplankton, she begins with a small sediment sample about the size of her fingertip. She then smears the sample on a glass slide. "When I look at it under a microscope, I can see thousands and thousands of fossils."

Marie-Pierre has looked at thousands of slides of nannoplankton fossils that are millions of years old. She recognizes some fossils right away. "There are species that are so familiar, they become like little friends. You know exactly what they can tell you." Planktonic forams and nannoplankton fossils can tell Tony when a layer formed.

Stopped Clocks Tell Time

If Bill or Marie-Pierre find several kinds of fossils in one sample, they know that sample came from a layer that formed at a time when all those plankton were alive. Then, Marie-Pierre and Bill can use that information to date sediment in a layer.

Thanks to fussy benthic forams, Tony can find out where a layer formed. And thanks to fossil "clocks," Tony can find out when a layer formed. He can use all this information to help him write the life history of the isthmus.

The Dating Game

Taken all together, information from benthic forams, planktonic forams, and nannoplankton gives Tony important clues about when and where a layer formed.

This shell is from a type of planktonic foram. This kind of foram lived from about 3.5 to 2.3 million years ago.

This shell is from a nannoplankton fossil. This kind of nannoplankton lived from about 8.6 to 2.6 million years ago.

This shell is from a benthic foram. It once lived in water about 100 to 600 meters (about 300 to 2,000 feet) deep.

If the three shells above were found in one rock layer, Tony would know that the layer formed 100 to 600 meters (about 300 to 2,000 feet) deep between about 3.5 and 2.6 million years ago.

4 The Closing Door

Swan Cay, at top, is a tiny island north of Bocas del Toro. Each dot on the map marks a site that Tony's team has visited to collect samples.

Laurie, Bill, and Marie-Pierre's forams and plankton give Tony information about when and where some layers formed. When he adds this information to a section, he can begin to see when and how that section rose out of the sea.

But each section tells the story of just one place on the isthmus. And even sections that are close together can have very different layers. The sections are like photographs that have fallen from the pages of an album. Tony has the pictures, but he doesn't know where they go in the album. How are the sections linked?

To find out, Tony lines up sections with layers that formed at the same time, but in different places. These layers were all on the seafloor at about the same time. With enough sections, Tony can make maps of coastlines at different times in the isthmus' history. When the maps are put in order, they show how the isthmus rose from the ocean.

Picture This

Tony collected samples from the part of Swan Cay shown inside the red box. He also drew sections of the area. Below is one of Tony's drawings. There is also a close-up of one part of the section.

Tony compared materials in the layers seen in the close-up with materials in the layers of other sections. The comparison showed that the layers seen in the close-up slowly tilted and fell over as the island rose from the ocean.

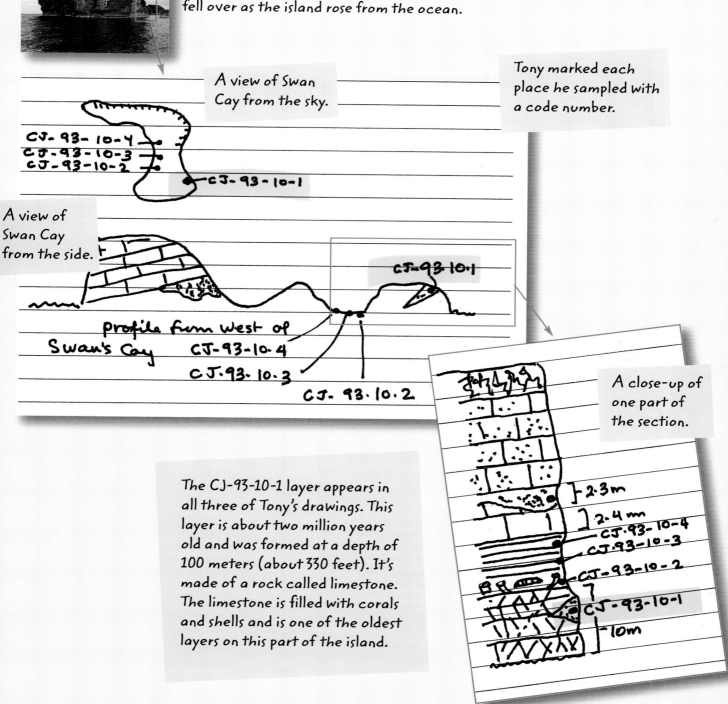

A view of Swan Cay from the sky.

Tony marked each place he sampled with a code number.

CJ-93-10-4
CJ-93-10-3
CJ-93-10-2
CJ-93-10-1

A view of Swan Cay from the side.

CJ-93-10-1

profile from west of Swan's Cay
CJ-93-10-4
CJ-93-10-3
CJ-93-10-2

A close-up of one part of the section.

2.3 m
2.4 m
CJ-93-10-4
CJ-93-10-3
CJ-93-10-2
CJ-93-10-1
10m

The CJ-93-10-1 layer appears in all three of Tony's drawings. This layer is about two million years old and was formed at a depth of 100 meters (about 330 feet). It's made of a rock called limestone. The limestone is filled with corals and shells and is one of the oldest layers on this part of the island.

Building a Bridge

Swan Cay is just one place Tony has studied. He has studied fossils in sections of places all over the isthmus. Tony uses the fossils to figure out the depth and time each layer in a section formed. He uses that information to make maps of the isthmus. This means Tony can pick a time and map how the isthmus looked at that time. For example, Tony can map the isthmus the way it looked 15 million years ago when some of its layers were on the seafloor. A series of these maps shows how the isthmus rose from the ocean.

15 Million Years Ago

About 15 million years ago, there was a deep ocean between North and South America. About 12 million years ago, the Pacific and North American plates bumped into each other. Volcanoes erupted to form a string of islands.

7 Million Years Ago

The volcanoes continued to erupt. Slowly, the islands rose as falling sediment piled up and as plates moved. The spaces between the islands also slowly filled with sediment.

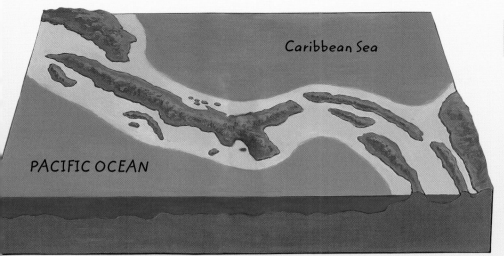

5 Million Years Ago

In time, the ocean flowed only through three narrow, shallow openings between the islands.

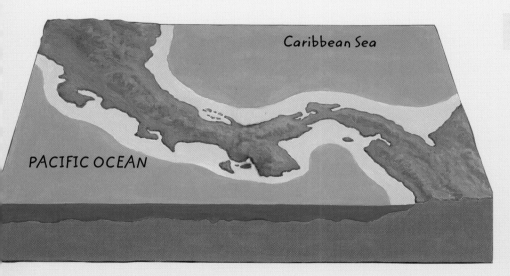

3 Million Years Ago

Finally, about 3 million years ago, the last bits of land rose above the water. The isthmus was born.

Tony's maps show that as North and South America moved together, the seafloor between them began to rise. At this time, the Atlantic and Pacific Oceans were still joined. A strong current moved from east to west through the opening between the continents.

Once the isthmus formed, a new set of changes began. One important change was the new direction in which ocean water began to move. Scientists can now trace how the isthmus formed. But for Tony and his team, the story is not finished.

Before and After

Most heat from the sun strikes Earth's surface near the equator. Ocean currents carry the heat around the world. When the isthmus closed, the currents changed direction.

The east-west current that moved between North and South America turned northward. This current became the Gulf Stream. It brings warm water to the shores of Europe and northern Russia. Because of the Gulf Stream, the water there never freezes in winter.

Changing Currents

Ocean water is always moving. As it warms, it rises. Then, it cools and sinks back down to the seafloor, where it begins to warm again. Wind pulls and pushes the water's surface. Earth's rotation spins the water.

One way water moves is in currents. Currents are strong flows of water. Larger currents have names, such as the Humboldt Current, the Alaskan Current, and the Labrador Current. Currents follow the same path over and over.

When the Atlantic and Pacific Oceans were joined, a strong current ran from the Atlantic to the Pacific. When the isthmus formed, it was as if a door had closed. The Atlantic and Pacific oceans

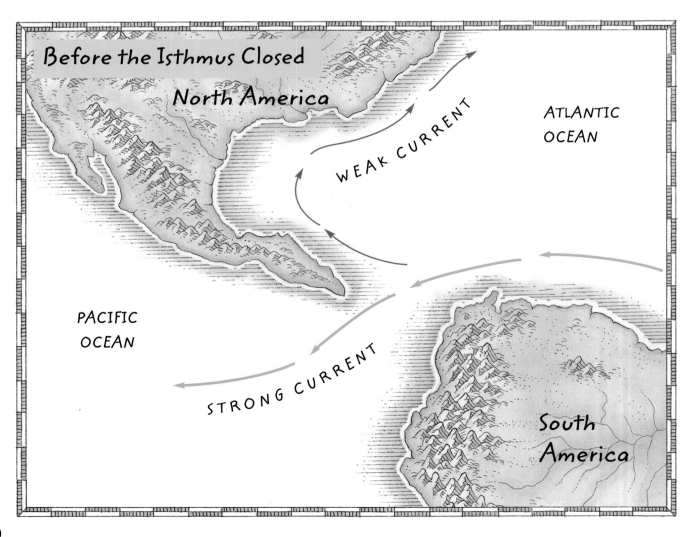

Before the Isthmus Closed

North America

WEAK CURRENT

ATLANTIC OCEAN

PACIFIC OCEAN

STRONG CURRENT

South America

were divided. The current that had run from east to west turned north. It moved along the eastern coast of North America. Today this current is called the Gulf Stream.

The Gulf Stream is a strong, warm current. It moves through the cold Atlantic Ocean. It mixes the water and warms everything around it. "The Gulf Stream stopped the sea from freezing along the coast of northern Europe. It probably formed the system of currents that joins the world's oceans," says Tony. "The Gulf Stream changed Earth's climates and the way the world works."

What happened to the world's animals and plants when the isthmus formed and the Gulf Stream began to flow north? Fossils tell the tale.

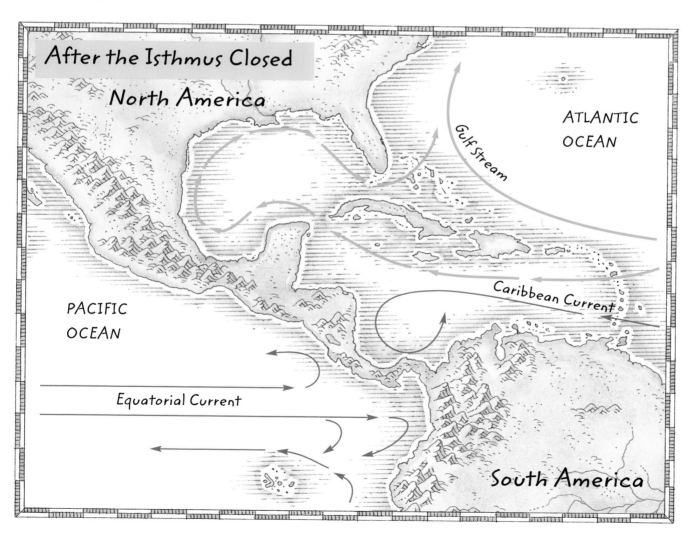

After the Isthmus Closed

North America

ATLANTIC OCEAN

Gulf Stream

PACIFIC OCEAN

Caribbean Current

Equatorial Current

South America

On one of their trips to Bocas, Steve and Nancy found corals in this cliff. The ancient corals were once underwater.

Ancient Corals

Tony, Nancy, and Steve stand on a cliff above the ocean. They are on Wild Cane Cay, a small island in Bocas. A thick layer of rock called sandstone is at the top of the cliff. Two million years ago, the layer was on the seafloor. It was covered in sea grass and dotted with groups of corals that grew as high as two feet.

Slowly, the layer rose. Since then, thousands and thousands of years of wind, sun, and rain have made the rock as smooth as a sidewalk. But here and there are rough lumps. These basketball-sized lumps are coral fossils.

Tony brought Nancy and Steve here to collect coral fossils. They hope the fossils will show them how the isthmus changed life in the oceans. Did the number and kinds of corals in the Atlantic and Pacific Oceans change? Did the new surroundings kill some kinds of corals and help others to grow?

If Tony and his team can understand what happened to the corals, they might learn more about what happened to other plants and animals. And what the team learns may help scientists predict, or tell, what will happen if the world changes in the future.

How Corals Live

Corals are small animals that live inside hard shells. Each shell is joined to another shell. Together the corals form colonies, and they grow where the water is clear. Colonies have different shapes. Some look like trees or reindeer antlers. Others look like brains or large rocks. When many colonies grow close together, they form a coral reef. Some reefs stretch for hundreds of miles. They can be bigger than the cities built by humans.

"Corals are a very special kind of animal," says Tony. "Reefs have to live in seas that are not too hot and not too cold. Corals live only at a certain depth and at a certain place." Coral reefs live best between sea level and 40 meters (about 130 feet) deep, where temperatures are between 15°C and 28°C (59°F and 82°F).

(above)
Scientists don't always chip fossils out with a hammer. Sometimes the stone is still soft. Then, they can use their fingers to pull out one- or two-million-year-old fossils.

(below)
These are fossils of ancient corals that are now extinct.

When the isthmus rose and divided the ancient ocean into two parts, the water around the isthmus changed. This change was important for corals. On the Atlantic side of the isthmus, the region called the Caribbean Sea became clearer, warmer, and saltier. These are the best conditions for corals.

On the Pacific side of the isthmus, the water became cloudier, colder, and less salty. Today there are fewer corals in the eastern Pacific Ocean than in the Caribbean Sea. And there aren't any kinds of corals that live on both sides of the isthmus.

Steve, Nancy, and Tony are collecting coral fossils at Bocas. Their work can help other scientists understand what can happen to plants and animals when Earth changes.

These are remains of a coral reef. Nancy and Steve found them on a collecting trip to Bocas.

Corals in the Past

On a single trip to Bocas, Nancy and Steve can collect hundreds of kilograms of coral fossils. It might take them about one year to measure and identify all the samples. Although Nancy and Steve still collect and study fossils, they have made some interesting discoveries already.

In the last four million years, the kinds of corals that live in the Caribbean Sea have changed. Before the isthmus closed, there were about 100 different kinds of corals. Today there are not so many. Only about 60 kinds of corals live in the Caribbean Sea and the Pacific Ocean near Panama.

About 80 of the 100 corals became extinct, but about 40 new kinds of corals appeared. All this happened in two quick bursts. One burst happened between three and four million years ago. This was when the isthmus was almost closed. The second burst of corals happened more than one million years later. By then, the Gulf Stream flowed north.

In both cases the changes had been happening for a long time. But it took a while for the living plants and animals to change, too. "It was as if the world stayed the same for millions of years, and then suddenly, many things happened in a hundred thousand years," Tony says.

Tony and his team still dig for fossils and study what they find. Tony is amazed by how much something as small as a land bridge can change life in the world's oceans. "It's a good example of how a very small change in one place can make a big difference to the world we live in," he says.

These pictures were taken near Panama. These corals don't live far from where Nancy, Tony, and Steve collect coral fossils.

Animal Parade

This is what the giant ground sloth *Megalonyx jeffersoni* might have looked like. Giant sloths traveled from South to North America across the isthmus. They roamed over the North American plains more than 10,000 years ago.

Tony and his team have found amazing fossils buried in the rock of the isthmus. They have found clams as big as baseballs, ancient sand dollars, and two-million-year-old shells so shiny they look new.

Tony has also found bones. In eastern Panama he found the bones of ancient animals that lived on land. These bones tell Tony that the isthmus caused other changes.

When the isthmus closed about three and one-half million years ago, it made a dam between two oceans. But it was also a bridge between two continents. For the first time in tens of millions of years, North and South America were joined. The isthmus became a bridge that animals used to travel between continents. It changed the wildlife in both places forever.

Strange Mammals of the Past

In the late 1700s, Thomas Jefferson received an unusual gift from a friend. It was a fossil of a giant claw. Thomas Jefferson, who was a paleontologist as well as a president of the United States, studied the strange fossil. He thought the claw came from a wild cat that was three times larger than a lion. He named the cat *Megalonyx*, or "great claw."

But Thomas Jefferson didn't have the remains of a huge cat. In fact, the animal was nothing like a meat-eating lion. It was a giant sloth, a cousin of the small, slow-moving sloths that live in tropical forests today. Big and slow, the giant sloth was almost two stories tall. It could walk on its hind legs like a gorilla, or it could walk on all fours. It was an herbivore, or an animal that eats plants. When it was hungry, it used its claws to tear down leaves from the branches of tall trees.

A Sudden Change

It is not surprising that Jefferson was wrong about the giant sloth. The animals that roamed North and South America millions of years ago were very different from the animals of today. It is hard to imagine what they looked like.

Gone but Not Forgotten

No one knows for sure what these ancient South American animals really looked like, but scientists can use fossils to make guesses.

Glyptodon ate grass, looked something like a tank, and was related to the armadillo.

Thylaco smilodon ate meat, carried its young in a pouch, and was about the size of a small tiger.

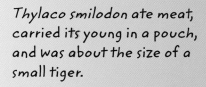

Astrapotherium is a mystery. Scientists think it may have lived part of its life in the water, like a hippopotamus, but they aren't sure.

All Alone

After Pangaea broke into pieces, South America drifted all alone. For 100 million years, its animals slowly changed. Over time the animals became different from the animals of any other continent.

When the isthmus formed, not all animals moved between the continents. Only animals that could live in places along the way could make the trip. Desert animals like this Marimachima, for example, didn't move to a new continent. Marimachimas are now extinct.

And the more fossils scientists find, the more questions they have. One of the biggest puzzles is that there are signs of a sudden change in the numbers and kinds of animals that lived on both continents. Nancy and Steve have evidence of the same kind of change in corals. But on land, the changes involved animals as small as mice and as big as mammoths. Today this change is called the Great American Interchange.

The Interchange Begins

Eight million years ago, the first land animals crossed the opening between North and South America. Only good swimmers crossed successfully. These swimmers were ancestors of modern raccoons and sloths. The sloths crossed from South America to North America. The raccoons moved in the opposite direction, from North America to South America.

For the next five million years, no land animals crossed at all. Tony says the current was much too strong. It must have been impossible for animals to swim across.

Once the land bridge formed, the Great American Interchange began. Animals started to move across in both directions. One of the first North American animals to move south was an ancestor of the modern peccary, a furry animal that looks like a pig. One of the first South American animals to move north was a kind of porcupine.

All kinds of animals traveled between the continents. Going south were mice, saber-toothed cats, and panthers. There were also deer, bears, horses, and mastodons. Anteaters marched to the north. So did sloths as big as elephants and armadillos as big as cars. There were even large "Terror birds" with beaks like axes.

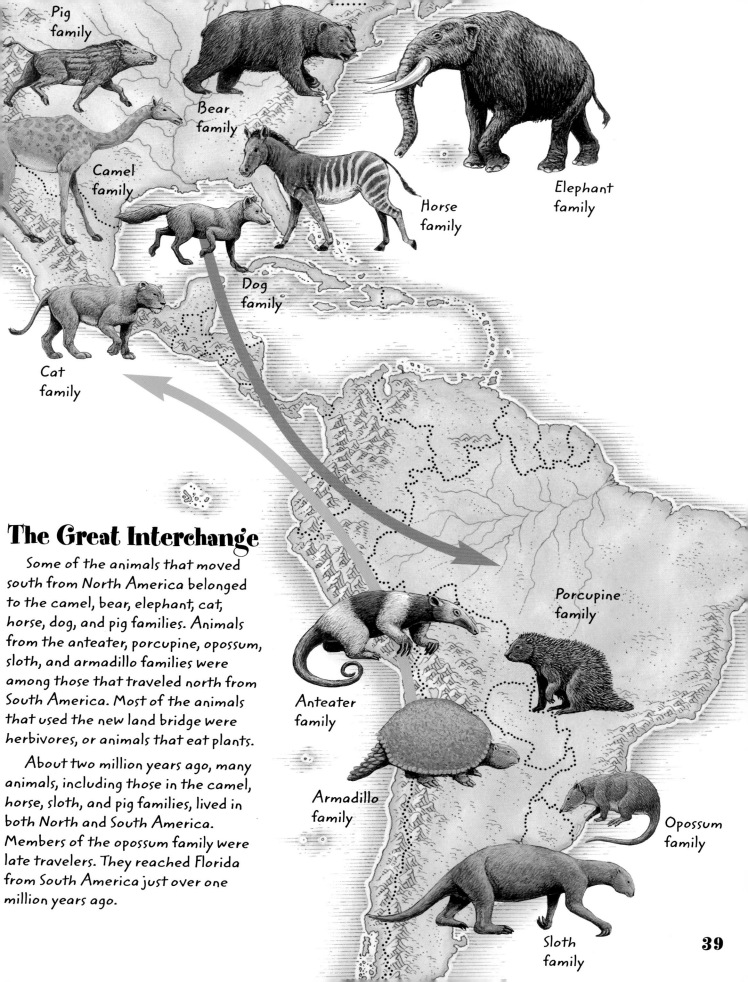

Pig family

Bear family

Camel family

Horse family

Elephant family

Dog family

Cat family

The Great Interchange

Some of the animals that moved south from North America belonged to the camel, bear, elephant, cat, horse, dog, and pig families. Animals from the anteater, porcupine, opossum, sloth, and armadillo families were among those that traveled north from South America. Most of the animals that used the new land bridge were herbivores, or animals that eat plants.

About two million years ago, many animals, including those in the camel, horse, sloth, and pig families, lived in both North and South America. Members of the opossum family were late travelers. They reached Florida from South America just over one million years ago.

Anteater family

Porcupine family

Armadillo family

Opossum family

Sloth family

The Great American Interchange lasted about one million years. Then, about one and one-half million years ago, the land bridge closed for most animals. The Amazon rain forest, with its thick plants and heavy rainfall, spread northward. Rain forest animals that could cross the bridge and move north didn't go all the way north. They needed to live where it was warm and wet. They followed the spreading jungle up into Central America.

The End of the Giants

At times in Earth's history, snow and ice have covered large parts of continents. These times are called Ice Ages. The last Ice Age happened about 19,000 years ago. It lasted until about 11,000 years ago. Suddenly, the largest animals in North and South America became extinct. They disappeared, leaving scientists today with a mystery. What became of these animals?

Some scientists have a theory, or explanation, for the mystery. They say humans killed the giant animals. Humans had crossed into Alaska during a time called the Great Ice Age. They moved across North America. Perhaps on the way, they killed the animals for food.

Other scientists don't agree. Human hunters would have used spears and arrows. If humans killed the animals, their tools would be found with the animals' fossils, but they are not.

One traveler from South to North America was Titanus walleri, or "Terror bird." It was more than 3 meters (about 12 feet) tall with sharp claws, long legs, and a bone-crushing beak. The first North American Titanus fossil was found at the bottom of a Florida river by scuba divers from the Florida Museum of Natural History. The bone was so big that scientists first thought it was part of a dinosaur.

Some scientists think that fast changes in the climate killed the giant animals. But others argue that climate changes would have killed smaller animals, too. Plus, this wasn't the first climate change. The climate had changed several times before without killing the giant animals.

A third theory says that disease killed the giants. But David Webb, a paleontologist at the Florida Museum of Natural History, doesn't agree. "I think this is a difficult theory to test," he says. "Whichever story you like, the clues are thin." David says that it's hard to find one cause for so many extinctions.

Those Who Made It

During the Great American Interchange, some animals lived better than others in their new homes. Animals from the south didn't do as well as animals from the north. Only three kinds of South American animals still live in North America. They are the armadillo, porcupine, and opossum.

The story in South America is different. Two-thirds of the animals that live in South America today have northern ancestors. They include deer, mice, raccoons, panthers, weasels, cats, dogs, and bears. Even some northern animals that no longer live in North America still live in South America. The best known example is the llama, an animal that has come to represent the South American mountains.

(above)
One of the Interchange's most puzzling mysteries is the great success of mice. Before the Interchange there was not a single mouse in South America. Today there are more than 60 kinds. David Webb, a paleontologist, calls it "an explosion of mice."

(below)
The llama is one of the most important South American mountain animals. But its ancestors came from North America. Llamas are distant cousins of desert camels. They are strong and can carry heavy loads for miles without drinking any water.

(above)
David Webb studies fossil "puzzle pieces" like these fossilized mammoth bones from Colombia's Aucilla River. He wants to know why some animals in the Great American Interchange succeeded and others didn't.

(below)
This is an artist's picture of what a mammoth might have looked like in Central America about 16,000 years ago.

David says there are no firm clues to explain why more animals from North America were successful in their new homes. He thinks one reason may be that animals from South America had lived for hundreds of years on an island continent that held very few carnivores, or meat-eating animals. Northern animals had learned to watch out for carnivores that traveled south at the same time they did. The southern herbivores had not learned to be careful. Many of them may have been eaten.

But no one knows the answer to the mystery for sure. David says it can be fun to look at the clues and ask, "How can this be?" or "Why? Is there something more?"

The Isthmus Changed the World

There are still hidden surprises in the isthmus' layers. But the layers have already told us a lot. We know how the isthmus changed the world. It formed the beautiful waters of the Caribbean Sea. It gave rise to the rich fishing grounds in the Pacific Ocean. It gave animals in North and South America a way to mix. It changed the way water moves in the world's oceans. And it made Europe's climate warmer.

The fossils in the isthmus help us understand the past. They may also help us understand the future. Tony says, "By looking at what happened in the past, you can better tell what might happen in the future." But Tony has another reason for studying fossils in the layers of the isthmus: "It's just fascinating."

The isthmus will continue to change in the years to come as Earth's plates move. Tony says that the isthmus will become more curved. He also thinks that part of the Gulf of Panama will fill in as the floor of the isthmus slowly rises from the sea.

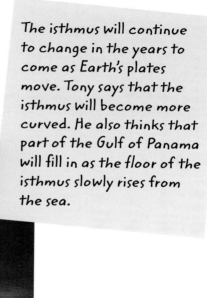

Glossary

benthic A word that means living at the bottom of an ocean, sea, or lake.

carnivore An animal that eats meat.

continents The seven main pieces of land on Earth. The continents are Africa, Antarctica, Asia, Australia, Europe, North America, and South America.

coral A simple animal that lives in the sea and is surrounded by a stonelike skeleton. The word is also used to describe just the skeleton.

core The center of Earth.

crust The thin, outer layer of Earth. The crust is the part of Earth that we walk on.

current A strong flow of water.

extinct No longer living. A species that no longer exists is extinct.

foraminifera (forams) Tiny animals that have shells and live in the world's oceans.

fossils The remains, such as skeletons or footprints, of ancient plants or animals.

geologist A scientist who studies the history of Earth, what it's made of, and how it formed.

Gulf Stream A strong, warm current that flows northeast from Cape Hatteras, North Carolina, to Newfoundland, Canada.

herbivore An animal that eats plants.

isthmus A thin piece of land that joins two larger pieces of land.

lava Rock that is so hot it becomes a thick liquid. Lava flows out of the Earth through a volcano.

layer In geology, one thickness of rock.

mantle The layer of Earth just above the core.

nannoplankton Very, very tiny floating plants.

paleontologist A geologist who studies fossils.

Pangaea The supercontinent that, about 260 million years ago, was made up of all seven continents as one land mass.

plankton Tiny animals and plants that drift or float in the world's oceans.

planktonic A word that means drifting or floating.

plate A section of Earth's crust.

plate tectonics A theory that describes how the parts of Earth's crust move.

reef Many colonies of coral growing close together. A reef rises near or above the surface of the water and may stretch for hundreds of miles.

section In geology, a picture of rock layers.

sediment Sand, fine soil, or mud that has not yet become solid rock.

Further Reading

Eldredge, Niles, Douglas Eldredge, and Gregory Eldredge. *The Fossil Factory: A Kid's Guide to Digging Up Dinosaurs, Exploring Evolution, and Finding Fossils.* Reading, MA: Addison-Wesley, 1989.

English, Peter. *Panama in Pictures* (Visual Geography Series). Minneapolis, MN: Lemer Publications Co., 1987.

Fagan, Elizabeth G., ed., *Children's Atlas of Earth Through Time.* Chicago, IL: Rand McNally & Co., 1990.

Harris, Nicholas, and Marc Gave. *Journey to the Center of the Earth.* Pleasantville, NY: Readers Digest, 1999.

Levy, Matthys, and Mario Salvadori. *Earthquake Games: Earthquake and Volcanoes Explained by 32 Games and Experiments.* New York, NY: M.K. McElderry Books, 1997.

Malin, Stuart. *Story of the Earth.* Mahwah, NJ: Troll Associates, 1991.

VanCleave, Janice Pratt. *Janice VanCleave's Earth Science for Every Kid: 101 Easy Experiments That Really Work.* New York, NY: John Wiley & Sons, 1991.

Index

Acknowledgments

The author would like to thank Marie-Pierre Aubry, Bill Berggren, Nancy Budd, Steve Cairns, Laurie Collins, John Dawson, Lucien Ferrenbach, Xenia Guerra, Lulu Ferrenbach, David Webb, Tony Coates (of course), and most of all, Gail Davidson.

Turnstone Publishing Group would like to thank Tony Coates for helping to create and review this book and Gloria Zelaya for her help with the book.

Credits:

Photographs courtesy of Tom Gidwitz except for the following:
Animals, Animals/Bisceglie, Michael: 41 bottom; Bybell, Dr. Laurel: 25 middle; Collins, Dr. Laurel S.: 20-21, 22, 24, 25 bottom, and all forams on pages 4, 12, 20, 23, 26, 36; Corbis: 17 middle; Guerra, Marcos/STRI: 13 upper right; Johnson Space Center/NASA: 43; Kleindinst/WHOI: 23 finger; NOAA/National Geophysical Data Center: 16 top; Norris, Dr. Richard: 25 top; Photo Researchers/Dalton, Stephen: 41 top; Strauch, Dr. Wilfried: 4 main image; Tom Bean, 1995/Tom Bean Photography: 17 top; United States Geological Survey: 16 middle; Urriola, Raineldo/STRI: 35; Webb, Dr. David S.: 42 upper left; Woods Hole Oceanographic Institution: 17 bottom.

Illustrations on pages 2, 14, 16, 17, 18, 19, 28, 29, 36, 37, 38, 39 animals, 40 and 42 are by Greg Wenzel.

Illustrations on pages 3, 5, 7, 15, 30, 31, and 39 background map are by David Stevenson.

Illustrations on pages 13, 26, and 27 are by Tony Coates.